D1643558

To

Giancarlo, giorno
della tua cresima 21-5-20..

Ti auguriamo che 'I doli..
ti guarda e benedice
ogni passo del tua camm..

From Nonno e Nonn..
XXX

Pocket Prayers
for Children

Pocket Prayers
for Children

**compiled by
Christopher Herbert**

illustrations by
Christina Forde

The National Society
*Leading Education
with a Christian Purpose*
Church House Publishing

National Society/Church House Publishing
Church House
Great Smith Street
London SW1P 3NZ

ISBN 0 7151 4911 3

Published 1999 by The National Society and Church
House Publishing

Cover design by Julian Smith
Printed by University Printing House, Cambridge

Contents

For Robin and Kerry Herbert
with love and enormous gratitude

Introduction

I have very much enjoyed putting this collection of prayers together. You will see that there is a great variety here – some are very old and use traditional language, others are very new; some are written by children, others by famous people. What they all have in common is a desire to speak to God from the heart, with love and truth.

When the disciples of Jesus, almost two thousand years ago, asked him to teach them to pray, he replied with words that have become one of the most precious and treasured prayers in the world: the Lord's Prayer. This collection uses the phrases of the Lord's Prayer to provide a framework for each of the sections.

I hope that through using these prayers, but above all by using the Lord's Prayer, you will draw closer and closer to God and will come to know the depths of his love and his unending kindness and mercy.

✠ *Christopher Herbert*
Bishop of St Albans

How to use this book of prayers

The most important thing to realize when you pray is that God loves you. Prayer begins in his love and ends in his love. He wants us to come to him just as we are and talk to him in complete trust and honesty.

One of the best ways of praying is to find somewhere quiet and then be as still as you can for a few minutes, knowing that you are in the presence of God. Once you have become still, talk to God, either out loud or in the secret depths of your own heart, using your own words. Then you could turn to one or more of the prayers in this book to see if they can help you find the words for the things you also want to say. When you have said all your prayers, try being still again for a minute or two, just resting on God's love, and then end your prayers by saying the Lord's Prayer.

In this way you may establish a pattern for your prayers (silence; prayer in your own words; silence; the Lord's Prayer), which will be a real strength to you, not only now, but in the years that lie ahead.

Unless otherwise stated, all the prayers in this anthology were composed by Christopher Herbert.

The Lord's Prayer

Traditional version

Our Father, who art in heaven,
hallowed be thy name;
thy kingdom come;
thy will be done;
on earth as it is in heaven.
Give us this day our daily bread.
And forgive us our trespasses,
as we forgive those who trespass against us.
And lead us not into temptation;
but deliver us from evil.

For thine is the kingdom, the power, and the
   glory,
for ever and ever. Amen.

The Lord's Prayer

Contemporary version

Our Father in heaven,
hallowed be your name,
your kingdom come,
your will be done,
on earth as in heaven.
Give us today our daily bread.
Forgive us our sins
as we forgive those who sin against us.
Lead us not into temptation
but deliver us from evil.

For the kingdom, the power, and the glory
  are yours
now and for ever. Amen.

Our Father

There is not a single person,
not a single bird,
not a single blade of grass
which is outside your love, O Lord;
for you give life to everything,
and for your humility and power
we give you thanks and praise.

God bless all those that I love;
God bless all those that love me;
God bless all those that love those that I love
and all those that love those that love me.

New England sampler

Our Father ————————

Bless, O God, our families;
give to those who care for us
the spirit of understanding and the spirit
   of love
that our homes may be places of peace
   and of laughter
for Jesus' sake.

Holy and loving God
open our eyes to see you,
open our minds to trust you;
open our hearts to love you
this day and for evermore.

Thank you, God, for Kissy my dog when she
   was alive –
and letting me use her as a step to get onto
   the sofa.
Thank you, God, for my brother, Mackenzie.

Chelsea Pemberton Whiteley (age 6)

Lord God and heavenly Father,
you promised that you would come to us;
be with us in the silence of our hearts,
in the depths of our imagination,
at the centre of our lives,
and fill us with your love, now and for
   evermore.

Our Father ————————————

Father, as those first shepherds knelt
   at the cradle,
   may we kneel quietly before you
just because we love you –
our most loving God and our most
   humble king.

Let all the world, O Lord,
come to know that you are our father,
our mother, our sister, our brother;
and through knowing you
may we then become
the family you would have us be,
for Jesus' sake.

O God, so beautiful;
O God, so holy;
O God, so loving
that you should die on a cross
for everyone and for me
is more than I can understand.
I come to you in the mystery of prayer
knowing that every day
you are bringing me closer
to your heart
and to your heaven,
through Jesus Christ, your Son, our Lord.

In heaven

Alleluia! Praise the Lord from the heavens,
praise him in the heights.
Praise him, all you angels of his,
praise him, all you his host.
Praise him, sun and moon,
praise him, all you shining stars.
Praise him, heaven of heavens,
and you waters above the heavens.
Let them praise the name of the Lord,
for he commanded and they were created.
He made them stand fast for ever and ever,
he gave them a law which shall not pass
    away.
Praise the Lord from the earth,
you sea-monsters and all deeps;
Fire and hail, snow and fog,
tempestuous wind, doing his will;
Mountains and all hills,
fruit trees and all cedars;
Wild beasts and all cattle, creeping things
    and winged birds;
Kings of the earth and all peoples,
princes and all rulers of the world;

Young men and maidens,
old and young together.
Let them praise the name of the Lord,
for his name is exalted,
   his splendour is over earth and heaven.
He has raised up strength for his people
   and praise for all his loyal servants,
the children of Israel, a people who are near
   him. Alleluia!

Psalm 148: Celebrating Common Prayer

Lord, you bathe the world with light;
bathe our hearts and our lives
with your peace, your love and your beauty
for ever.

In heaven

When the sun is setting
and the sky changes colour very, very slowly
and with great beauty,
accept our quiet joy as a prayer of
thanksgiving to you,
our Lord and our God.

Lord,
the sun is full of energy
making seeds grow,
bringing us life.
Make us like the sun,
radiant with the glory of being alive
for Jesus' sake.

Lord God,
  you are the king of the universe,
king of creation
and king of glory; we worship you on this
  kingly day.

The light of Christ pierces the darkness
  like a sword;
the light of Christ engulfs the darkness
  like a fire;
the light of Christ conquers the darkness
  like a victorious army.
O light of Christ,
shine in our hearts and lives
and bring us your life and your eternal victory.

In heaven ————————————

O most holy and most loving God,
surrounded by the songs of angels
and the laughter of saints,
grant us to know your presence
here on earth,
that we may enjoy you
now and for ever.

O king, all glorious –
shine into the depths of our hearts
with the brilliance of your love,
that our lives may be filled with the peace
of your most holy presence.

Glorious God,
radiant with light,
vibrant with love;
let our lives be so open to your presence
that we may share, even now,
in the joy and beauty of heaven,
for Jesus' sake.

Hallowed be
your name

God, you are our father and our mother,
   the life in all that exists;
thank you for the gift of your wonderful
   world,
for the gift of ourselves,
for the gift of other people
and for all whom we love.

Thank you, Lord, for all the rainbows of the
   world:
the rainbows in flowers,
the rainbows in streets,
the rainbows in traffic,
the rainbows in faces.
We praise and bless you, O holy God,
for a rainbow-full world.

———— *Hallowed be your name*

Lord Jesus,
you are alive in our world:
alive in peals of laughter,
alive in the joy of love,
alive in the heart of music,
alive in the power of sunlight,
alive in the breath of life,
alive in the prayers
at the centre of our souls.
Lord Christ,
living Lord,
let us share in your most holy life,
now and for ever.

Hallowed be your name ───────

Dear God in heaven,
you are so beautiful,
so glorious,
so good,
that when I try to think about you
my mind reaches its very limits;
then all I can do is to thank you with all my
   heart
just because you are who you are.

Night is drawing nigh.
   For all that has been – Thanks.
To all that shall be – *Yes.*

Dag Hammarskjöld 1905–61

Lord, we thy presence seek,
   May ours this blessing be;
Give us a pure and lowly heart,
A temple meet for thee.

John Keble 1792–1866

——— *Hallowed be your name*

Glory to thee, my God, this night
   for all the blessings of the light;
keep me, O keep me, king of kings,
beneath thy own almighty wings.

Thomas Ken 1637–1711

Dear God,
I have stopped worrying about the bad
   things
and I've been thinking all about the good
   things in life
because I've been thinking about you.
Thank you. Amen.

Abigail Gouldbourne (age 7)

Hallowed be your name ———

God, you listen to me.
When I need help, you listen to me.
When I need comfort, you listen to me.
When I need guidance, you listen to me.
When I need love, you love me.

Becky Perrins (age 12)

'I am': probably the most simple thing you
    said
but probably the most memorable.
It explains you so much –
how you said 'I am' to Moses from the
    burning bush
and everyone knew who you were,
that's because you're the only I am.

Kathryn Cockroft (age 12)

———— Hallowed be your name

When the day returns,
call us with morning faces, and with
    morning hearts,
eager to labour,
happy if happiness be our portion,
and if the day is marked for sorrow,
strong to endure.

Robert Louis Stevenson (1850–94)

Lord, let thy glory be my end,
    Thy word, my rule
and then thy will be done.

King Charles I (1600–48)

Hallowed be your name ———

Dear God,
Thank you for the people who invented
  medicines,
like penicillin and vaccinations;
for all the medicines that stop you dying
  from things
like measles and smallpox and chickenpox.
Please allow people to make more medicines
until every single illness can be cured:
bacteria illnesses and virus illnesses.
I know you made all this amazing lovely
  universe
but I would like it if the dying rate could go
  down
very slowly, year by year. Amen.

Andrew Hood (age 6)

Your kingdom come

Father, you have made the world very
  beautiful.
Teach us to love our world
and to treat it with reverence and with care
for Jesus' sake.

These are the patterns we have found:
lichen on a stone, cobwebs on hedgerows,
words on paper . . .
Pattern our lives with your colours of love,
dear God,
that we may be beautiful for you.

Your kingdom come ———————

We hold up to you, God, all the poor on
    the earth;
may we who are rich, share our wealth,
we who are well fed, share our food,
we who are educated, share our learning,
so that in our own small way
we may take part in the coming of your
    kingdom.

Lord, let your Holy Spirit rest upon our
    school
that it may be a place of love and truth,
where the weak are made strong
and the strong learn humility,
and all of us learn the wisdom
that alone comes from you.

Your kingdom come

Lord God,
let your peace rest so gently on our hearts
    and minds
that we may have the strength
to work for peace in our world,
today, tomorrow and for ever.

O God, our heavenly Father, whose Son,
our Lord Jesus Christ,
took the form of a servant and became the
    Man for others,
give us the same spirit of service
and help us to follow in his steps,
that with love and humility
we may give ourselves to those who need
    our help,
for the glory of your name.

Frank Colquhoun

Your kingdom come ————

Lord Jesus Christ
   risen from the tomb
your love is let loose in the world;
let your love conquer my heart
that I may become one of your disciples
and follow you for ever.

Lord, make me an instrument of your peace:
where there is hatred, let me bring your love;
where there is injury, pardon;
where there is discord, union;
where there is doubt, faith;
where there is despair, hope;
where there is darkness, light;
where there is sadness, joy;
for your mercy's sake.

Attributed to St Francis of Assisi (1182–1226)

Lord, you are love,
Lord, you are peace,
Lord, you are our gentle strength.
You are with us wherever we go
so we need not be afraid.
For your love, your peace and your strength
we thank you, now and always.

Your will be done, on earth as in heaven

When I wake up in the morning,
thank you, God, for being there.
When I go to school each day,
thank you, God, for being there.
When I am playing with my friends,
thank you, God, for being there.
And when I go to bed at night,
thank you, God, for being there.

Almighty God, Father of all mankind,
in your Son, you took upon yourself the
  sorrow of the world.
We offer you our own sorrow and sadness,
knowing that you will help us to bear
  our grief
through the infinite understanding and love
of Jesus Christ our Lord.

Your will be done, on earth as in heaven

O God, I thank you
for all the creatures you have made,
so perfect in their kind –
great animals like the elephant and the
    rhinoceros,
humorous animals like the camel and
    the monkey,
friendly ones like the dog and the cat,
working ones like the horse and the ox,
timid ones like the squirrel and the rabbit,
majestic ones like the lion and the tiger,
for birds with their songs.
O Lord, give us such love for your creation
that love may cast out fear,
and all the creatures see in us
their priest and friend;
through Jesus Christ our Lord.

George Appleton (1902–93)

Your will be done, on earth as in heaven

Lord Christ, shine upon all
who are in the darkness of suffering and
    grief,
that in your light, they may receive hope
    and courage
and in your presence, may find their rest
    and peace,
for your love's sake.

Alan Warren

There are some old people whose lives are
    like autumn:
mellow, quiet and wise.
Help us, Lord, to learn from them
and to listen to them patiently.

Your will be done, on earth as in heaven

O loving Father,
I offer myself to be used by you
for the comforting of the sad,
the strengthening of the weak
and the befriending of the lonely,
through Jesus Christ, our Lord.

Let all the world in every corner sing
My God and King!
The heavens are not too high,
his praise may thither fly.
The earth is not too low,
his praises there may grow.
Let all the world in every corner sing,
My God and King!

George Herbert (1593–1632)

Your will be done, on earth as in heaven ————————

Christ has no body now on earth but yours,
no hands but yours, no feet but yours;
yours are the eyes
through which to look with Christ's
   compassion on the world,
yours are the feet
with which he is to go about doing good,
and yours are the hands
with which he is to bless us now.

St Teresa of Avila (1515–82)

Lord Jesus,
You suffered so much pain and cruelty on
   the cross
But through it all, you held on to love.
Be with us whenever life is very, very tough
and keep us loving, no matter what happens –
for that is your way,
the way that leads to peace and truth.

Your will be done, on earth as in heaven

Dear God,
protect all the creatures of the world:
from the tiny money spider on his web
to the huge blue whale in the deep blue ocean,
from the gentle manatee in the Florida
    Everglades
to the fierce tiger in the Indian jungle,
from the slow sloth in the South American
    rain forest
to the speedy cheetahs on the African plain.
This world you have made, with all its
    different habitats,
is such a wonderful place.
Care for us and all the creatures
who share this beautiful world. Amen.

Matthew Swan (age 10)

Your will be done, on earth as in heaven ──────────

Dear Lord,
Let kindness get to people's hearts like a
    raindrop
on a spider's web.
Let all the bad things, like drugs, get washed
    away by love.
Let all the young people grow up to be good
and honest, and help them not to lead a life
of crime.
Lord, in your mercy,
hear my prayer.

Hannah Holt (age 9)

Dear God,
Look after everyone we love.
Help me with my tests this week.
Help me to get my Capitals in the right place.
Help Buttons, my dog, to be brave for his
    injections.
Amen.

Philip Lewis (age 7)

Give us today our daily bread

Like a seagull gliding on the wind,
may we trust ourselves to your love,
   O Lord.

Blessed are you, Lord our God, king of the
   universe,
who feeds the entire world in his goodness –
with grace, with kindness and with mercy.
He gives food to all life, for his kindness is
   eternal . . .
Blessed are you, God, who nourishes all.

Jewish Grace

Give us today our daily bread –

The bread is pure and fresh,
the water is cool and clear.
Lord of all life, be with us.
Lord of all life, be near.

African Grace

God is great,
God is good,
let us thank him for this food.

Anon

God is with me now.
God sees me.
God hears me.
God smiles at me.
God loves me.
God wants me –
now and always.

From St Saviour's Priory

– Give us today our daily bread

Lord, you are our hope and strength,
staying with us in trouble,
walking with us in danger
and comforting us in our sadness.
Keep us always mindful of your love
that we may be strong and courageous
in all that we think and speak and do,
knowing that you are our closest and most
    loyal friend.

Give us big hearts, dear God,
big enough to embrace everyone,
big enough to say sorry,
big enough to be humble,
big enough for you.

Give us today our daily bread –

Eternal Light, shine into our hearts,
Eternal Goodness, deliver us from evil,
Eternal Power, be our support,
Eternal Wisdom, scatter the darkness of
   our ignorance,
Eternal Pity, have mercy on us;
that with all our heart and mind and soul
   and strength
we may seek your face and be brought by
   thine infinite mercy
to thy holy presence; through Jesus Christ
   our Lord.

Alcuin of York (AD 735–804)

Bless with your wisdom and patience,
dear God,
the farmers of the world,
that they may work with you and your
   creation
for the good of us all.

– Give us today our daily bread

Our prayer, dear Lord,
is that we shall do something to feed the
   hungry
and shall work for justice in our world,
through Jesus Christ our Lord.

Bread is a lovely thing to eat –
   God bless the barley and the wheat,
A lovely thing to breathe is air –
God bless the sunshine everywhere.
The earth's a lovely place to know –
God bless the folks that come and go!
Alive's a lovely thing to be –
giver of life – we say – bless thee.

Anon

Give us today our daily bread –

Make us worthy, Lord,
To serve our fellow men throughout the
   world
who live and die in poverty and hunger.
Give them, through our hands, this day their
   daily bread,
and by our understanding love, give peace
   and joy.

Mother Teresa of Calcutta (1910–97)

Forgive us our sins

Lord, we hold up to you those people who
   are violent.
We don't want to pretend that we aren't
   violent at times;
so, Lord, here we are –
puzzled by others and puzzled by ourselves.
Please make sense of us and show us
the way of peace.

Hands who touched the leper,
touch my wounded heart;
hands who healed the blind man,
heal my aching soul;
hands who cured the lame,
mend my disjointed life;
hands who embraced all life,
enfold me in your peace.
Lord, merely touch and heal,
cure and forgive.

Anon

Forgive us our sins ————

O Lord Jesus, we confess
that we are sometimes deliberately unkind to
   other people.
Forgive us and help us to show them your
   love.

Heavenly Father,
   your light overcomes darkness;
take everything in my life that is dark
and transform it into glory;
through Jesus Christ our Lord.

Forgive us our sins

Peter promised that he would stay with you
    always, Lord,
and then he abandoned you
and felt ashamed.
I know that I might have done the same –
and so, as you forgave Peter,
giving him the courage to proclaim your
    resurrection,
forgive me when I abandon my friends
and give me the courage to say I'm sorry
to them
and to you.

O God, full of love, hear my prayer.
If we have done things which shame us,
show us the right way.
Thank you for your love which surrounds us
    each day
and goes with us into the peace of night.

Anon

Forgive us our sins ——————

In the darkest moment of our lives, O God,
    remind us that you are light,
you are hope,
you are love.

Dear God,
Why do I get cross when I lose my pocket
    money?
Why do I feel jealous when my friends get
    lots of presents?
Why do I get pleased when my sister gets
    told off?
Why do I feel sad when I have too many
    toys?
I hope you understand me, and I'm very,
    very sorry.
Amen.

Alice Taylor (age 8)

Dear God,
Where did we go wrong?
What have we done to your wonderful world?
Why is it that some have plenty, while others
  have none?
Why do we start wars, killing lots of people?
What is the reason for birth and death?
What is the purpose of this place, this world,
  Earth?
Only you know these things. Amen.

Amanda Partridge (age 11)

Lamb of God, you take away the sins of the world:
have mercy on us.
Lamb of God, you take away the sins of the world:
have mercy on us.
Lamb of God, you take away the sins of the world:
grant us peace.

Ancient Greek Prayer

43

As we forgive those who sin against us

When your friends betrayed you, Lord,
you took their sins upon yourself
and forgave them.
Please forgive us when we betray those we love
and when we betray you,
for without your forgiveness
our lives will become bitter and sad.
We are sorry, O God;
O God, please forgive.

Drop thy still dews of quietness,
till all our strivings cease;
take from our souls the strain and stress,
and let our ordered lives confess
the beauty of thy peace.

John Greenleaf Whittier (1807–1892)

As we forgive those who sin against us

Incline us, O God!
  to think humbly of ourselves,
to be saved only in the examination of our
  own conduct,
to consider our fellow creatures with kindness,
and to judge of all they say and do
with the charity which we would desire from
  them ourselves.

Jane Austen (1775–1817)

Lord, increase our understanding
  of ourselves, of each other, of you;
through the power of your Holy Spirit
and for the sake of your kingdom,
this day and always.

As we forgive those who sin against us ———————

O Divine Master,
Grant that I may not so much seek
To be consoled, as to console,
To be understood, as to understand,
To be loved, as to love,
For it is in giving that we receive;
It is in pardoning that we are pardoned;
And it is in dying that we are born to eternal
  life.

St Francis of Assisi (1182–1226)

As we forgive those who sin against us

On that Good Friday, Lord,
they tried everything.
They tried to quench your love with insults,
to drown your love in jeering,
to kill your love
by nailing you to a cross.
But your love was not to be beaten.
You forgave them their insults,
you forgave them the jeering,
you forgave them the piercing;
and in your forgiveness
your love conquered all
and rose into new and eternal life.
For your ceaseless and most patient love
we give you thanks and praise,
our wounded and most holy Saviour.

As we forgive those who sin against us ─────────

Dear Lord,
  I would like to talk.
How do you become friends with someone
who doesn't like you particularly?
There is a girl in my class who likes all of my
    friends
but I get the impression she doesn't like me.
Should I feel hurt?
Should I talk to her?
Should I try to ignore it?
I don't know and I just thought you might
    know.
I know you will care and answer me. Amen.

Charlotte Dyer (age 9)

Lead us not into temptation

Thank you, heavenly Father,
for those who risk their lives
in storms and great dangers
to bring others to safety.
When they are frightened, protect them;
when they are in peril, comfort them
and give them at all times
your peace and your strength, for Jesus' sake.

The sea sweeps up the beach
   and laps around the sandcastles
until they crumble and fall.
On the farther side of the beach,
near the cliff,
the sea dashes against the rocks
and they stand firm and strong.
Help us, at all times, O Lord,
to be more like the rock than sand.

Lead us not into temptation —

The things, good Lord, that we pray for,
give us the grace to labour for.

Thomas More (1478–1535)

God give us grace to accept with serenity
   the things that cannot be changed,
courage to change the things that should
   be changed,
and the wisdom to distinguish the one
   from the other.

Reinhold Niebuhr (1892–1971)

— Lead us not into temptation

Save us, O Lord, waking,
   and guard us, sleeping,
that awake we may watch with Christ
and asleep we may rest in peace.

From the Service of Compline

O Father in heaven,
when I am confused
and do not know what I should do,
give me, deep in my heart,
the knowledge I need,
and then the courage
to put that knowledge into action,
through Jesus Christ our Lord.

Lead us not into temptation —

Lord Jesus Christ,
   when you were put to the final test
you did not flinch
but, with undaunted courage,
walked the way of the cross;
give us, we pray, the desire
and the courage
to follow your way of love,
each and every day,
for your name's sake.

O God,
   you know me better than I know myself;
when I face temptation,
give me strength to overcome,
but if I fail,
be merciful, I pray,
for the sake of your Son,
Jesus Christ our Lord.

But deliver us from evil

Almighty God,
who gave your only Son to die for the sins of
   the world;
have mercy on all who are tempted
and on all who, through weakness or wilfulness,
fall into sin;
reveal to them your gracious love,
that turning to you for help,
they may be led into fellowship with you
and obedience to your will;
through Jesus Christ our Lord.

Dear Father,
When I am scared
and I think monsters are going to come,
help me not to think that;
because I know they're not, if you are there.
Amen.

Wesley Wrigley (age 6)

But deliver us from evil ———

Dear Lord Jesus,
help all those children who are in sadness
because of divorce with their parents.
Make them feel loved,
even without one of their parents,
by your love.
Bless the mothers and fathers as well;
make them realize
what is happening to their family. Amen.

Rebecca Toms (age 10)

———— *But deliver us from evil*

Dear God,
I hope you can hear me,
lots of fighting and war is going on below you.
The thing I would really like to say is
help us to start again
and so this time we would know what would
   happen
if we destroy it and it will be a complete misery.
Help not just my family
but other families too who have split up.
Please help split up families (especially with
   children)
because I am in a very hard position at the
   moment
because my mum and dad have split up.

Sometimes I think to myself
it seems that me and my sister are right
   stuck in the middle
and I can't get out.
Please help us to create peace
and to love and care.

But deliver us from evil ———

I expect you are feeling very sad;
I would help if I could
but I am only one person out of thousands of
    people
and it would be hard to let everybody know;
so I just can't help.
I'll have to go now, speak to you later.

A young girl (age 8)

I bind unto myself today
the power of God to hold and lead,
his eye to watch, his might to stay,
his ear to hearken to my need;
the wisdom of my God to teach,
his hand to guide, his shield to ward,
the word of God to give me speech,
his heavenly host to be my guard.

St Patrick (389–461)

—— *But deliver us from evil*

Dear Lord,
I would just like to say what a changing place
the world is starting to be.
Ever since the Dunblane incident, for example,
I, and many others, have become worried
  and shaky
about lots of things.
Whenever I'm on my own, I feel insecure,
and if a parent or guardian isn't there
to pick me up when I've finished an activity,
I start to worry.
I would just love it if there was nothing
to worry about in the world.
So please, God, help me
and everyone else
to stay confident and not to worry;
through Jesus' name. Amen.

Matthew Neville (age 11)

But deliver us from evil ———

Father in heaven,
when the darkness threatens to overwhelm us
and we are very afraid,
be with us in your love,
and banish from our hearts and minds
all the terrors and evil of the world,
and then enfold us in your peace,
for Jesus' sake.

For the kingdom

Lord in heaven, you have promised us new life
through your Son, Jesus Christ;
help us to live with that promise
in our hearts and in our lives,
so that our sadness can be turned by you
into blessing and strength in the days ahead.

Dear Lord,
thank you for football,
for the fun of it:
slide tackles, overhead kicks,
and diving and long shots;
for the skill of it:
passing accurately,
dribbling, kick ups and volleys;
for the joy of it
when you score a goal.
Good football is excellent.
Thank you, God, for football.

Shaun Kemp (age 8)

For the kingdom ────────

In the silence
  The deep, echoing silence
I listen for You.

In the dark
The calm, tranquil dark
I listen for You.

In the storm
The howling, raging storm
I listen for You.

In the waves
The crashing, ravening waves
I listen for You.

By the stream,
The tumbling, bubbling stream
I listen for You.

In the woods
The cool, shady woods
I listen for You.

For the kingdom

And in the calm and the quiet
The power and the noise
The serene and the busy
I listen
And You are there.

Frances James (age 12)

O holy God, you have made our world very
   curious;
help me, as I explore your world,
to discover your presence in all things,
for Jesus' sake.

Be thou my vision, O Lord of my heart,
Be all else but naught to me, save that thou art,
Be thou my best thought in the day and the
   night,
Both waking and sleeping, thy presence my
   light.

Traditional Irish hymn

For the kingdom ——————

Eternal God and Father,
  by whose power we are created
and by whose love we are redeemed,
guide and strengthen us by your Spirit,
that we may give ourselves to your service
and live in love to one another and to you,
through Jesus Christ our Lord.

Joint Liturgical Group

O most loving God,
you are at the very centre of all life
and embrace the universe with your love;
open our eyes to see you,
our minds to know you,
and our hearts to love you –
this day, and for evermore.

The power

Morning glory, starlit sky,
Leaves in springtime, swallows' flight,
Autumn gales, tremendous seas,
Sounds and scents of summer night;

Soaring music, tow'ring words,
Art's perfection, scholar's truth,
Joy supreme of human love,
Memory's treasure, grace of youth;

Open, Lord, are these, Thy gifts,
Gifts of love to mind and sense;
Hidden is love's agony,
Love's endeavour, love's expense.

Love that gives, gives ever more,
Gives with zeal, with eager hands,
Spares not, keeps not, all outpours,
Ventures all, its all expends.

Drained is love in making full;
Bound in setting others free;
Poor in making many rich;
Weak in giving power to be.

The power

Therefore He Who Thee reveals
Hangs, O Father, on that Tree
Helpless; and the nails and thorns
Tell of what Thy love must be.

Thou art God; no monarch Thou
Thron'd in easy state to reign;
Thou art God, Whose arms of love
Aching, spent, the world sustain.

W. H. Vanstone

The water comes crashing down the mountain,
turning waterwheels, driving turbines,
giving us energy for our work and our play.
Come to us, O Lord, in your power
and fill our lives with the energy of your Holy
   Spirit
that we may bring life to others.

Dear God,
thank you for my happy life.
Amen.

Olivia Powell (age 4)

Dear Father God,
thank you for making me.
I can dance and I can run.

Amy Dale (age 5)

Ah, the fragrance of new grass!
I hear his footsteps coming –
the Lord of the resurrection.

Jiro Sasaki, Bishop of Kyoto

The power

All your works praise you, O Lord,
and your faithful servants bless you.
They make known the glory of your kingdom
and speak of your power;
That the peoples may know of your power
and the glorious splendour of your kingdom.
Your kingdom is an everlasting kingdom,
your dominion endures throughout all ages.
The Lord is faithful in all his words
and merciful in all his deeds.
The Lord upholds all those who are bowed
  down.
The eyes of all await upon you, O Lord,
and you give them their food in due season.

Psalm 145.10–16: Celebrating Common Prayer

Be still, for the presence of the Lord, the Holy
    One, is here;
come, bow before him now, with reverence
    and fear.
In him no sin is found, we stand on holy
    ground.
Be still, for the presence of the Lord, the
    Holy One, is here.

Be still, for the glory of the Lord is shining all
    around;
he burns with holy fire, with splendour he is
    crowned.
How awesome is the sight, our radiant King
    of Light!
Be still, for the glory of the Lord is shining all
    around.

Be still, for the power of the Lord is moving in
    this place,
he comes to cleanse and heal, to minister his
    grace.

The power ────────────────

No work too hard for him, in faith receive
   from him;
be still, for the power of the Lord is moving in
   this place.

David J. Evans (b.1957)

. . . and the glory are yours

Mountains are very still,
they just sit and sit.
They point to your greatness, O God,
silent and quiet.
Help me to be still and silent,
like a mountain;
sitting still, listening to your voice.

Timothy King

O God, Creator of Light,
at the rising of your sun this morning,
let the greatest of all lights,
your love,
rise like the sun within our hearts.

Prayer of the Armenian Apostolic Church

. . . and the glory are yours —

Father of love, make us like gleaming mirrors
so that we may reflect your glorious light.

In the soaring beauty of our cathedrals, O
    God,
let your simple presence dwell,
that we may come close to you in holiness
and in your holiness, find our peace;
for Jesus' sake.

— . . . and the glory are yours

Dear Lord,
I pray for all those people who are scared of
    the dark
and feel darkness inside them.
Please help them to battle through the
    nothingness
of the night.
It is lonely in the dark
and people sometimes don't feel your
    presence.
Please help those people
to feel that you are there.
When we are scared
please help us.
Thank you for helping us
by giving us the gift of life.
You are the light of the world.
Help us see, Lord. Amen.

Christopher Clayton (age 10)

. . . and the glory are yours —

Lord,
make me like a mirror
facing the place where the sun always
    shines,
so I can reflect the joy of the sun
on to all of the people.

Lauren Newman (age 8)

Now and for ever. Amen.

When words fail me, Lord,
   and I don't know what to make of things,
help me to be really silent, deep-down silent,
and wait in trust for the answers.

Alone with none but thee, my God,
I journey on my way.
What need I fear when thou art near
O king of night and day?
More safe am I within thy hand
than if a host did round me stand.

St Columba (AD 521–97)

Now and for ever. Amen. ———

Draw us nearer to you each day, O Lord,
for you are our purpose and our destiny.

May the road rise to meet you.
   May the wind always be at your back.
May the sun shine warm upon your face,
the rain fall soft upon your fields,
   and until we meet again,
may God hold you in the palm of his hand.

Traditional Celtic blessing

——— *Now and for ever. Amen.*

O Father, all time is in your hands.
May we hold on to that which is good from
   the past,
to be aware of the joys of the present
and rejoice in the endless promise of the
   future.

I know, O God,
that wherever I travel,
you will be with me.
There is nowhere I can go,
nothing I can face
which is beyond your love and strength.
And so I place myself
into your care and keeping,
knowing that at all times
and in all places,
I am in your hands.

Now and for ever. Amen. ——

Word of God, give me the words
  To praise you for ever and ever.

Jesus Christ, thou child so wise
Bless mine hands and fill mine eyes
And bring my soul to Paradise.

Hilaire Belloc

—— *Now and for ever. Amen.*

Be thou a bright flame before me,
Be thou a guiding star above me,
Be thou a smooth path below me
And a kindly shepherd behind me,
Today – tonight – and for ever.

St Columba (AD 521–97)

The Lord bless us and keep us,
   the Lord make his face to shine upon us,
and be gracious unto us;
the Lord lift up the light of his countenance
   upon us,
and give us peace.

Traditional blessing, based on Numbers 6.24 –6

—— *Now and for ever. Amen.*

God, let your blessing rest upon us
like dew on the grass,
bringing refreshment, beauty and peace
to body, mind and soul.

Lord, keep us safe this night,
secure from all our fears.
May angels guard us while we sleep
till morning light appears.

Anon

God be in my head, and in my understanding;
God be in my eyes, and in my looking;
God be in my mouth, and in my speaking;
God be in my heart, and in my thinking;
God be at my end, and at my departing.

The Sarum Primer 1558

Index of first lines

Thank you, God, for Kissy my dog, 5
Thank you, heavenly Father, 49
Thank you, Lord, for all the rainbows of the world, 14
The bread is pure and fresh, 34
The light of Christ pierces the darkness like a sword, 11
The Lord bless us and keep us, 77
The sea sweeps up the beach, 49
The things, good Lord, that we pray for, 50
The water comes crashing down the mountain, 64
There are some old people whose lives are like autumn,
    28
There is not a single person, 3
These are the patterns we have found, 21
We hold up to you, God, all the poor on the earth, 22
When I wake up in the morning, 26
When the day returns, 19
When the sun is setting, 10
When words fail me, Lord, 73
When your friends betrayed you, Lord, 44
Word of God, give me the words, 76

Index of authors and sources

Acknowledgements

The author and publisher gratefully acknowledge permission to reproduce copyright material in this publication. Every effort has been made to trace and contact copyright holders. If there are any inadvertent omissions we apologise to those concerned and will ensure that a suitable acknowledgement is made at the next reprint.

The Archbishops' Council: The Lord's Prayer (modified traditional version) from *The Alternative Service Book 1980* is reproduced by permission. The Lord's Prayer in its modern form is adapted from the International Consultation on English Texts (ICET) version (pp. 1-2).

The European Province of the Society of St Francis: Psalms 145 (p. 66) and 148 (p. 69) from *Celebrating Common Prayer*, 1992.

Faber & Faber Ltd: 'Dear God in heaven' from Dag Hammersköld, *Markings*, 1964 (p. 16).

Joint Liturgical Group: 'Eternal God and Father' (p. 62).

Kingsway's Thankyou Music: 'Be still, for the presence of the Lord' by David J. Evans. Copyright © 1986 Kingsway's Thankyou Music. PO Box 75, Eastbourne, East Sussex BN23 6NW, UK. Used by kind permission (p. 67).

Mowbray, an imprint of Cassell plc: 'O God, our heavenly Father' by Frank Colquhoun (p. 23); 'Lord Christ, shine upon all' by Alan Warren (p. 28) from David Silk, *Prayers for Use at the Alternative Services*, 1980, 1986.

Oxford University Press: 'O God, I thank you' by George Appleton from *The Oxford Book of Prayer*, 1985 (p. 27).

SPCK: 'Make us worthy, Lord' by Mother Teresa of Calcutta from Robert Runcie and Basil Hume, *Prayers for Peace*, 1987 (p. 38).

W. H. Vanstone: 'Morning glory, starlit sky', copyright © James William Shore, from W. H. Vanstone, *Love's Endeavour, Love's Expense*, Darton, Longman & Todd, 1977 (pp. 63–4).

Prayers by Christopher Clayton (p. 71), Kathryn Cockroft (p. 18), Amy Dale (p. 65), Charlotte Dyer (p. 48), Abigail Gouldbourne (p. 17), Hannah Holt (p. 32), Andrew Hood (p. 20), Frances James (p. 61), Shaun Kemp (p. 59), Philip Lewis (p. 32), Matthew Neville (p. 57), Lauren Newman (p. 72), Amanda Partridge (p. 43), Becky Perrins (p. 18), Olivia Powell (P. 65), Matthew Swan (p. 31), Alice Taylor (p. 42), Rebecca Toms (p. 54), Chelsea Pemberton Whiteley (p. 5), Wesley Wrigley (p. 53) and A young girl (p. 56) are prize-winning entries of the 1998 *Together for Children* prayer competition and are reproduced by permission.

The National Society
A Christian Voice in Education

The National Society (Church of England) for Promoting Religious Education supports everyone involved in Christian education – teachers, school governors, students, parents, clergy, parish and diocesan education teams – with the resources of its RE centres, courses, conferences and archives.

Founded in 1811, the Society was chiefly responsible for setting up the nationwide network of Church schools in England and Wales, and still helps them with legal and administrative advice for headteachers and governors. It was also a pioneer in teacher education through the Church colleges. The Society now provides resources for those responsible for RE and worship in any school, lecturers and students in colleges, and clergy and lay people in parish education. It publishes a wide range of books and booklets and a resource magazine, *Together with Children*.

The National Society is a voluntary body which works in partnership with the Church of England Board of Education and the Division for Education of the Church of Wales. An Anglican society, it also operates ecumenically, and helps to promote inter-faith education and dialogue through its RE centres.

For further details of the Society or a copy of our current resources catalogue and how you can support the continuing work of the Society, please contact: The National Society, Church House, Great Smith Street, London SW1P 3NZ, Telephone: 020 7898 1518, Fax: 020 7898 1493, Email: info@natsoc.c-of-e.org.uk

Web addresses: www.natsoc.org.uk
www.churchschools.co.uk